A New Life

This is the true life story of a young girl who had her life transformed from being timid and troubled with the infamous inferiority complex which threatened to affect every part of her life.
She miraculously comes in contact with the Word of God in a most unique and mind-blowing way.
Journey with Lydia and relive her true life testimony.

SOZO
TRUE LIFE TESTIMONIES

UNITED KINGDOM:
Unit C2, Thames View Business Centre, Barlow Way Rainham Essex, RM13 8BT.
Tel.: +44 (0)1708 556 604

USA:
8623 Hemlock Hill Drive Houston, Texas.77083
Tel: +1-281-759-5111;
     +1-281-759-6218

SOUTH AFRICA:
303 Pretoria Avenue Cnr.
Harley and Braam Fischer,
Randburg, Gauteng,
South Africa.
Tel.: +27 11 3260971
Fax.: +27 11 3260972

NIGERIA:
Plot 97, Durumi District,
Abuja.

NIGERIA:
LoveWorld Conference Center
Kudirat Abiola Way,
Oregun P.O. Box 13563 Ikeja,
Lagos.
Tel: +234-812-340-6791

CANADA:
4101 Steeles Ave W, Suite 204
Toronto, Ontario
Canada M3N 1V7

LoveWorld Publishing Limited
3, Adebayo Akande Street,
Oregun, Ikeja, Lagos Nigeria.
E-mail: info@kiddiesloveworld.org
Website: www.kiddiesloveworld.org
ISBN 978-1-950926-08-4

Copyright ©2019 LoveWorld Publishing.
All rights reserved under International
Copyright Law.

Contents and/or cover may not be
reproduced in whole or in part in any
form without the express written
permission of LoveWorld Publishing.

HAVE YOU EVER WISHED, THAT GOD COULD GIVE YOU A NEW LIFE? A LIFE FULL OF GLORY AND VITALITY!

FOR ME IT WAS A WISH COME TRUE!

WELL...! GOD ACTUALLY GAVE ME A BRAND NEW LIFE...

...AND I AM SURE YOU WOULD LIKE TO HEAR ABOUT IT...

OOPS! I DID NOT INTRODUCE MYSELF.

I AM LYDIA! ...MY STORY WILL HAVE TO TAKE US A FEW YEARS BACKWARDS...

...BACK TO WHEN I WAS MUCH YOUNGER THAN I AM NOW...

IT ALL BEGAN...

YOU SEE, IN A FAMILY OF FIVE SIBLINGS, I AM THE YOUNGEST...
...AND I HAD A CHRONIC STAMMERING CONDITION.
I-I-I-I N-NEED TO E-EAT T-T-THE...
ELEVEN YEARS AGO...
AS A TEENAGER, I USED TO FEEL INFERIOR ABOUT MY STATURE.
AS THOUGH NOT ENOUGH,I WASN'T SATISFIED WITH MY LOOKS...
"I WISH I HAD HER **FIGURE**. I WISH I HAD THOSE **BEAUTIFUL LEGS**, THOSE NICE SET OF **TEETH**."
...BUT IN SPITE OF ALL THAT, I DISCOVERED THAT GOD HAD PUT **TALENTS** IN ME.
I BELIEVE I CAN FLY..I BELIEVE I CAN TOUCH THE SKY....
I COULD **SING**.
I COULD WRITE CREATIVE STORIES
...AND BEST OF ALL, I COULD **DRAW**!

EIGHT YEARS AGO...
IN MY SECONDARY SCHOOL, WHERE I ONCE ATTENDED...
AYO! AYO!! COME NOW!!!
YES
...I HAD A LOVE FOR THE SCIENCES, SO I JOINED THE SCIENCE CLASS...
...YET I BELIEVED SOMEHOW, I WOULD TURN OUT AN **ARTIST**.
BUT I DIDN'T KNOW HOW.
I WAS TOLD BACK THEN, THAT ARTISTE IN MY COUNTRY, NEVER WENT FAR IN LIFE.
SO, I WAS KIND OF IN A DILEMMA. I WAS CLUELESS ABOUT MY FUTURE.
MY DAD SAYS ARCHITECTS GET RICH VERY FAST.
NAH! IN OUR COUNTRY, ARTIST DON'T GO FAR IN LIFE!
YES, THERE'S A LOT OF MONEY IN ARCHITECTURAL WORKS.
I'M SURE IT'S THE SAME WITH OTHER COURSES, LIKE FINE ART.
NOT UNLESS YOU HAVE CONNECTION.
IS IT BETTER I BECOME A PHARMACIST AND EARN ENOUGH MONEY, THAN TO BE AN ARTIST?

AFTER MY "O" LEVELS EXAMINATION, I STILL DIDN'T KNOW WHAT I WANTED TO BE IN LIFE.
WHAT DO I DO ABOUT THIS..?
I WANT TO BE AN ARTIST!
HEY! I DON'T WANT TO BE A LAWYER, I WANT TO BE AN ENGINEER...!
AN ENGINEER? WHY? I WANT TO BE A SCIENTIST!

TWO YEARS LATER...
MY BROTHERS USED TO TALK ABOUT THE SECOND COMING OF JESUS CHRIST...
IN THIS LIFE, ONE HAS TO BE SERIOUS WITH GOD.
...THIS GOT MY ATTENTION, AND MY HEART WAS FLOODED WITH THOUGHTS...
THAT'S TRUE! WITH ALL YOUR DREAMS AND PURSUIT OF SUCCESS...,
..YOU JUST MIGHT NOT BE WALKING IN GOD'S WILL.
I REMEMBER THE BIBLE SAYS SOMETHING ABOUT THE LAST DAYS...
...ABOUT JESUS' SECOND COMING AND THOSE WHO WOULD BE LEFT BEHIND.
WHAT IF I DON'T MAKE IT TO HEAVEN?
...FOR DAYS I COULD NOT SLEEP RIGHT, MY THOUGHTS WERE LIKE WILD FIRE IN MY HEAD...!
WHAT IF I AM LEFT BEHIND?
I DON'T WANT TO BE TORTURED BY THE DEVIL.
GOD, LET ME BE BORN AGAIN BEFORE I GAIN ADMISSION INTO THE UNIVERSITY.
I DON'T WANT TO FALL INTO THE WRONG HANDS.
AT THIS TIME, MY FATHER AND MOTHER HAD GIVEN THEIR LIVES TO CHRIST JESUS...
HOLY BIBLE
...AND SO HAD MY SISTER. MY BROTHERS AND I WERE THE ONLY ONES LEFT, WHO HAD NOT BEEN SAVED.

MY SISTER TOO HAD A WONDERFUL STORY OF HER OWN..
...SHE WAS MINISTERED TO BY SOME CHRISTIANS.
SHE GAVE THEM RAPT ATTENTION WHILE THEY SPOKE...
SISTER PRINCESS. JESUS LOVES YOU AND WANTS TO HELP YOU
YES! JESUS WILL GIVE YOU A NEW LIFE. A FRESH START!
SHE WAS ALSO GIVEN A SPECIAL GIFT, THAT IS, A COPY OF RHAPSODY OF REALITIES, A DAILY DEVOTIONAL.
IMMEDIATELY AFTER CHURCH, SHE BEGAN TESTIFYING ABOUT HER SALVATION TO EVERYONE.
SHE WAS INVITED TO CHURCH WHERE SHE GAVE HER HEART TO CHRIST
I RECEIVE JESUS AS MY LORD
...I COULD FEEL IT, THERE WAS A CHANGE IN MY SISTER. I WANTED THAT CHANGE...!
I FEEL A CHANGE IN ME. A SUDDEN PEACE.
WOW!!!
THAT IS GREAT!

...ONE AFTERNOON, WHILE I WAS IN THE ROOM WITH MY ELDER SISTER...
PRINCESS! COULD I ASK YOU A QUESTION?
...STUDYING THE RHAPSODY OF REALITIES DEVOTIONAL, I ASKED HER A QUESTION...
HOLY BIBLE
PRINCESS, WHEN WILL THE NEXT ALTAR CALL BE MADE IN CHURCH?
THIS COMING SUNDAY
DO YOU WANT TO GIVE YOUR HEART TO JESUS CHRIST?
YES!
I AM HAPPY FOR YOU.
THANKS

IT WAS TWO SUNDAYS LATER, ON THE 8TH OF JULY 2007 THAT I GAVE MY HEART TO JESUS CHRIST.
...THE PASTOR LEAD ME TO JESUS CHRIST, HE ASKED ME TO SAY THESE WORDS AFTER HIM...
SAY THIS AFTER ME, "O LORD GOD, I COME TO YOU IN THE NAME OF JESUS...
...THOSE WORDS FLOODED INTO MY SOUL AND SPIRIT....
O LORD GOD I COME TO YOU IN THE NAME OF JESUS.
THAT MOMENT I RECEIVED JESUS CHRIST IN ME I KNEW I BECAME A CHANGED PERSON.
...NOW I KNEW I COULD FLY! THERE WAS THIS GLOW FROM WITHIN MY SPIRIT...SO SWEET! OH...SO WONDERFUL!
...FROM THEN ON I NOTICED A TRANSFORMATION IN MY LIFE!
THE PREACHER LAID HIS HANDS ON ME AND I RECEIVED THE HOLY SPIRIT. THE NEXT DAY, I STARTED SPEAKING IN TONGUES.

I KEPT SPEAKING IN TONGUES EVERYDAY...
BEFORE THIS TIME, I USED TO BE **SHY** AND **TIMID** BECAUSE **OF** MY **STAMMERING**.
WHICH OF YOU, CAN TELL ME THE FORMULA FOR THIS EQUATION?
maths
4 + 4 = 8
10 + 10 = 20
20 + 20 = 40
COMMUNICATING AT SCHOOL WAS A MATTER OF CONCERN FOR ME.
LYDIA JUST TOLD ME THE ANSWER.
WHY CAN'T SHE JUST ANSWER?
YOU KNOW SHE **STAMMERS**...!
I KNOW THE ANSWER! BUT I CAN'T GIVE THE ANSWER...! HOW DO I SAY IT?
SUDDENLY MY **STAMMERING** STOPPED! PRAISE GOD!
NOW I AM BOLD AND CAN **TALK FREELY** WITH ANYONE...
JESUS PAID THE PRICE FOR YOU.
YES! **JESUS** CAN GIVE YOU A NEW JOB! IF YOU TRUST HIM.

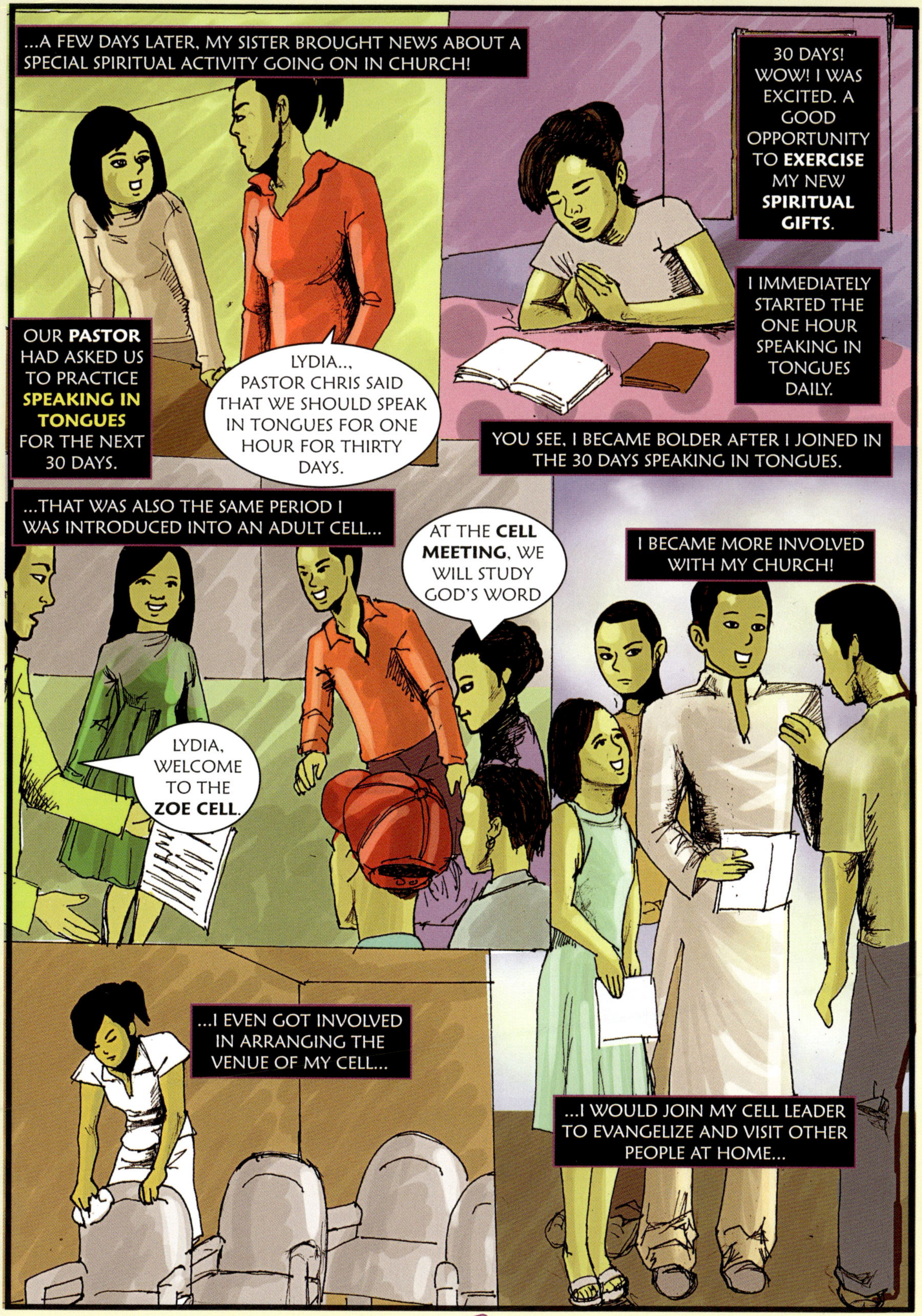

...A FEW DAYS LATER, MY SISTER BROUGHT NEWS ABOUT A SPECIAL SPIRITUAL ACTIVITY GOING ON IN CHURCH!
OUR **PASTOR** HAD ASKED US TO PRACTICE **SPEAKING IN TONGUES** FOR THE NEXT 30 DAYS.
LYDIA..., PASTOR CHRIS SAID THAT WE SHOULD SPEAK IN TONGUES FOR ONE HOUR FOR THIRTY DAYS.
30 DAYS! WOW! I WAS EXCITED. A GOOD OPPORTUNITY TO **EXERCISE** MY NEW **SPIRITUAL GIFTS**.
I IMMEDIATELY STARTED THE ONE HOUR SPEAKING IN TONGUES DAILY.
YOU SEE, I BECAME BOLDER AFTER I JOINED IN THE 30 DAYS SPEAKING IN TONGUES.
...THAT WAS ALSO THE SAME PERIOD I WAS INTRODUCED INTO AN ADULT CELL...
AT THE **CELL MEETING**, WE WILL STUDY GOD'S WORD
LYDIA, WELCOME TO THE **ZOE CELL**.
I BECAME MORE INVOLVED WITH MY CHURCH!
...I EVEN GOT INVOLVED IN ARRANGING THE VENUE OF MY CELL...
...I WOULD JOIN MY CELL LEADER TO EVANGELIZE AND VISIT OTHER PEOPLE AT HOME...

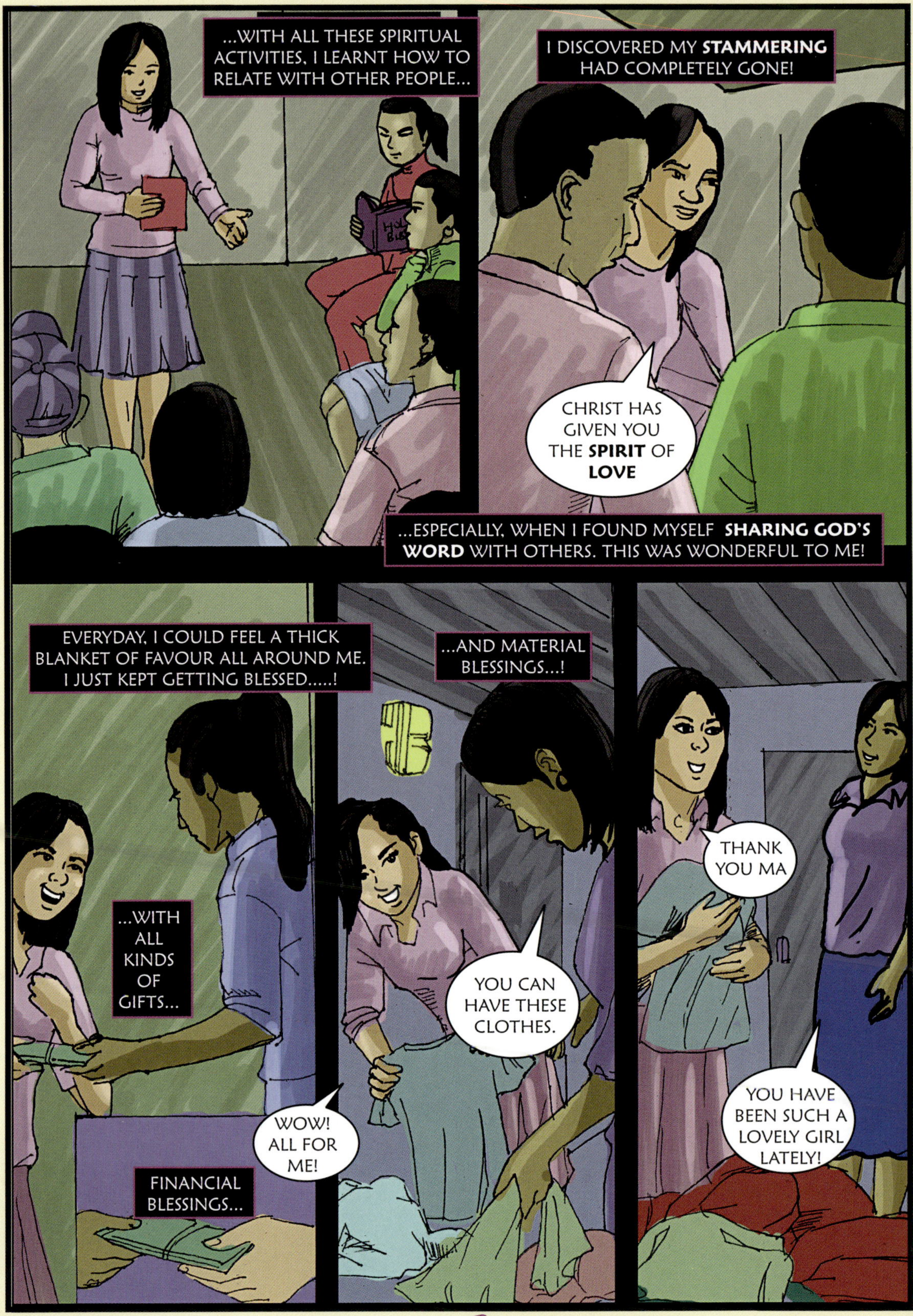

...WITH ALL THESE SPIRITUAL ACTIVITIES, I LEARNT HOW TO RELATE WITH OTHER PEOPLE...
I DISCOVERED MY **STAMMERING** HAD COMPLETELY GONE!
CHRIST HAS GIVEN YOU THE **SPIRIT** OF **LOVE**
...ESPECIALLY, WHEN I FOUND MYSELF **SHARING GOD'S WORD** WITH OTHERS. THIS WAS WONDERFUL TO ME!
EVERYDAY, I COULD FEEL A THICK BLANKET OF FAVOUR ALL AROUND ME. I JUST KEPT GETTING BLESSED.....!
...WITH ALL KINDS OF GIFTS...
FINANCIAL BLESSINGS...
WOW! ALL FOR ME!
...AND MATERIAL BLESSINGS...!
YOU CAN HAVE THESE CLOTHES.
THANK YOU MA
YOU HAVE BEEN SUCH A LOVELY GIRL LATELY!

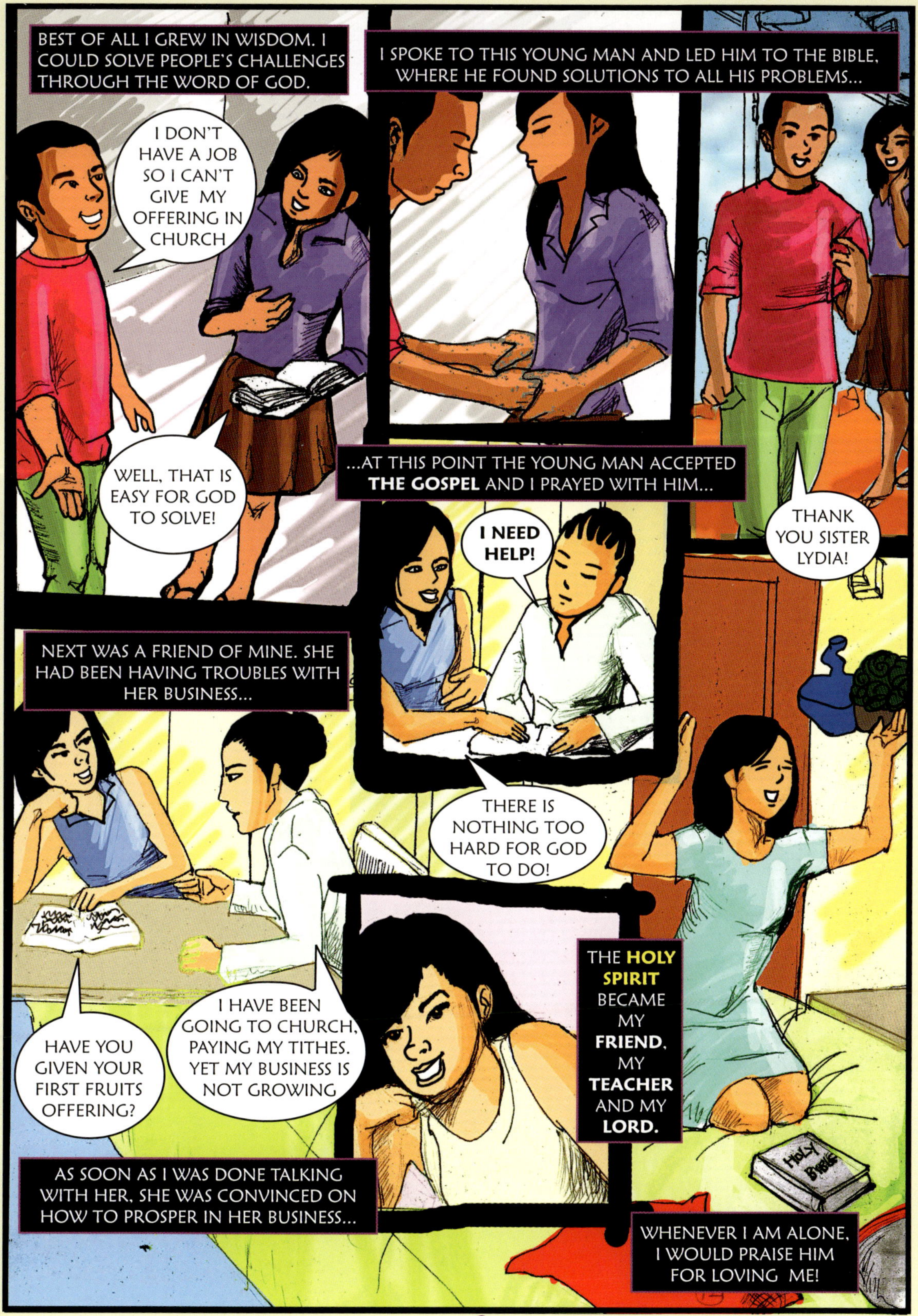
BEST OF ALL I GREW IN WISDOM. I COULD SOLVE PEOPLE'S CHALLENGES THROUGH THE WORD OF GOD.
I DON'T HAVE A JOB SO I CAN'T GIVE MY OFFERING IN CHURCH
WELL, THAT IS EASY FOR GOD TO SOLVE!
I SPOKE TO THIS YOUNG MAN AND LED HIM TO THE BIBLE, WHERE HE FOUND SOLUTIONS TO ALL HIS PROBLEMS...
THANK YOU SISTER LYDIA!
...AT THIS POINT THE YOUNG MAN ACCEPTED **THE GOSPEL** AND I PRAYED WITH HIM...
I NEED HELP!
THERE IS NOTHING TOO HARD FOR GOD TO DO!
NEXT WAS A FRIEND OF MINE. SHE HAD BEEN HAVING TROUBLES WITH HER BUSINESS...
I HAVE BEEN GOING TO CHURCH, PAYING MY TITHES. YET MY BUSINESS IS NOT GROWING
HAVE YOU GIVEN YOUR FIRST FRUITS OFFERING?
AS SOON AS I WAS DONE TALKING WITH HER, SHE WAS CONVINCED ON HOW TO PROSPER IN HER BUSINESS...
THE **HOLY SPIRIT** BECAME MY **FRIEND**, MY **TEACHER** AND MY **LORD.**
HOLY BIBLE
WHENEVER I AM ALONE, I WOULD PRAISE HIM FOR LOVING ME!

EVERY SUNDAY, I LEARNT SOMETHING NEW ABOUT THE HOLY SPIRIT.
CAST ALL YOUR CARES ON JESUS
THE HOLY SPIRIT CAME FROM JESUS TO HELP YOU IN LIFE.
THE HOLY SPIRIT CAN HELP YOU LOVE THOSE WHO DISLIKE YOU.
CAST ALL YOUR TROUBLES ON JESUS...
SO GOD WANTS ME TO FORGIVE BROTHER UCHE!
IN CHURCH, I WAS TAUGHT HOW TO EXTEND GOD'S LOVE TO OTHERS AROUND ME...!
Wow!! I LOVE JESUS
I WILL PUT THE WORD TO WORK TODAY!
HE USES ANYONE TO CORRECT ME IF I DO WRONG
HELLO MATT!
UCHE HAS ALWAYS BEEN RUDE TO ME, WHAT DO I DO TO HIM?
WELL UCHE NEEDS HELP, GOD CAN HELP HIM CHANGE.
ALL YOU NEED TO DO IS TO PRAY FOR HIM, AND HE WILL CHANGE HIS HABITS!
HELP HIM CHANGE BY LOVING HIM!
WHEN MATT LEFT, I THOUGHT OVER WHAT HE SAID AND I FELT FREE KNOWING I DON'T HAVE TO BE UPSET WITH UCHE ANYMORE.
I FORGIVE UCHE FOR ALL THE TIMES HE WRONGED ME!
NOW I KNOW WHAT IT IS TO LOVE!

...NOW I AM LIVING A LIFE FULL OF GRACE AND FAVOUR...

...NOW I DO NOT STAMMER ANYMORE...

...I HAVE BEEN INDEED TRANSFORMED BY THE WORD OF GOD.

THERE IS SO MUCH TO TELL YOU ABOUT THIS NEW LIFE

...I TALK LIKE I OWN THE WORLD...

IF YOU HAVE NOT GIVEN YOUR HEART TO CHRIST...

WHAT ARE YOU WAITING FOR?

JESUS LOVES YOU DEARLY

HE WANTS TO CHANGE YOUR **LIFE**!

...HE WANTS YOU TO BE THE **BEST** IN YOUR TIME!

DON'T WAIT TILL **NEXT** TIME

MAKE **JESUS** THE LORD OF **YOUR LIFE NOW**.

WHEN YOU DO, HE WILL BRING YOU INTO HIS FAMILY OF KINGS AND PRIESTS...

..JUST LIKE ME!

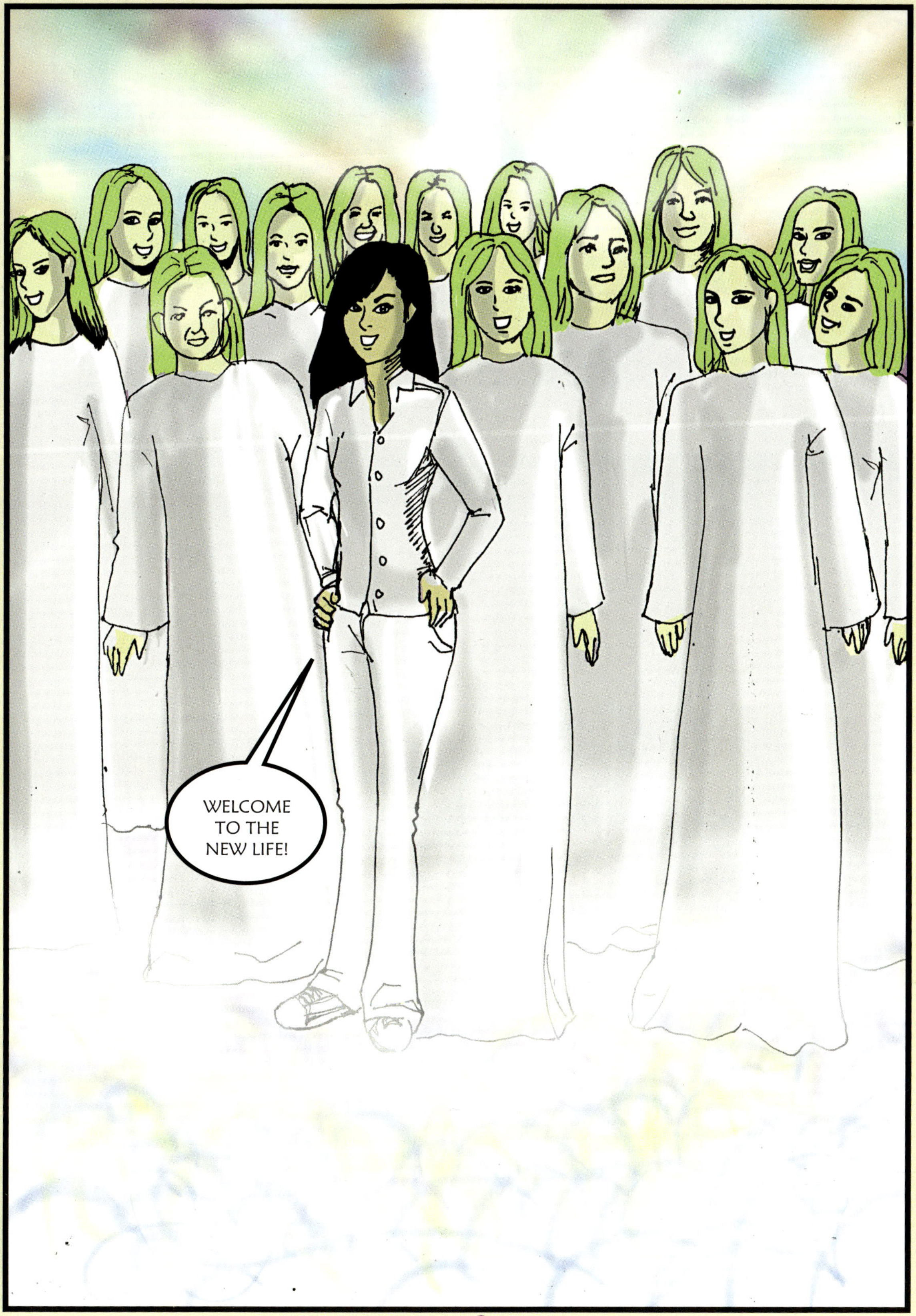
WELCOME TO THE NEW LIFE!

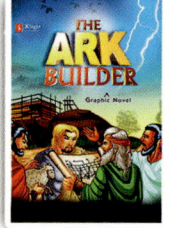

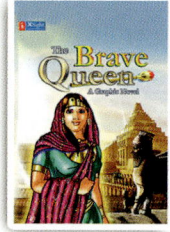

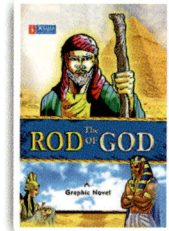

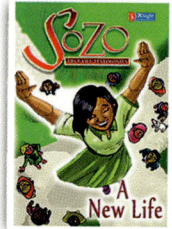

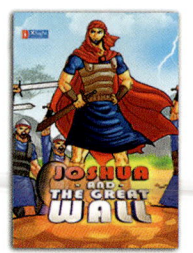

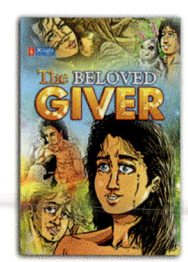

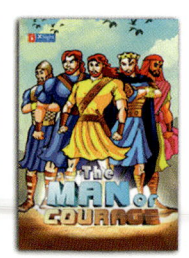

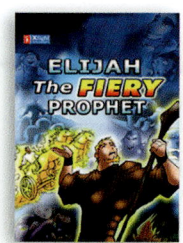

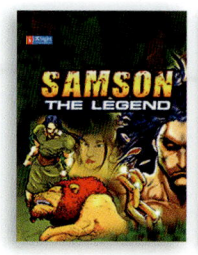

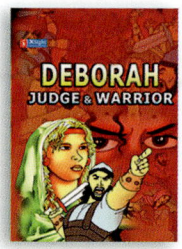

The real SUPERHEROES
unite in these extraordinary COMIC BOOKS & GRAPHIC NOVELS!

UNITED KINGDOM: Tel.: +44 (0)1708 556 604
USA: Tel: +1-281-759-5111; +1-281-759-6218
NIGERIA: Tel: +234-812-340-6791
SOUTH AFRICA: Tel.: +27 11 3260971.

XSight ENTERTAINMENT